Hinduism in words and pictures

Sarah Thorley
designed and illustrated by the author

CONTENTS

1. Religion in India p.2
2. Hindu beliefs p.4
3. Gods and goddesses p.6
4. Rama and Krishna p.10
5. Worship p.12
6. Temples p.14
7. At home p.16
8. Hindu families p.18
9. Samskara p.20
10. Pilgrimage p.22
11. Festivals p.24
12. Holy men p.26
13. Hindus in Britain p.28
Tasks p.31
Notes for teachers p.32

WORD LIST

Brahman   Hindu name for God. Brahman is the unseen Great Power, Great Spirit. (Not the same as Brahma, see p. 6, or Brahmin, see p. 19)

Sanskrit   ancient language in which the oldest Hindu scriptures are written

samsara   rebirth (or reincarnation). The Hindu belief that when your body dies, your soul is born again in the world into a new body

atman   Hindu word for soul or spirit. The part of you which is not your body or your mind

karma   the belief that your actions in this life will affect what your next life is like

moksha   freedom from the cycle of rebirth. When you have become so holy that at death your soul is not born again but becomes united with Brahman

dharma   sacred law. Religious duties for each person according to their caste and stage in life

caste   word for the different groups of people in Hindu society based on family and/or job

guru   teacher, spiritual guide (spiritual means to do with the soul and God)

arti   worship in which one or more lights (flames) are circled in front of a deity

puja   worship which includes offering gifts (food, flowers, money) to a deity

mantra   sacred verse or passage in Sanskrit which may be repeated to bring blessings

prashad   food offered to and blessed by the deities and then shared among the worshippers

mandir   place which houses the deities. It may be a big temple or a simple home shrine

darshan   sight of a deity or guru or being blessed by being in their presence

diva   small lamp lit with a wick soaked in ghee (melted butter) or oil

samskara   religious ritual to mark important points in a person's life

to bless   to make holy. Blessings are God's 'favours'

deity   god or goddess. Statues of the deities are called 'murti'

to fast   to go without certain foods for a period of time, for religious reasons

ritual   religious ceremony or activity which is always performed in the same way

shrine   sacred (holy) place with an image (picture, statue or carving) of one or more of the gods and goddesses, where people pray and worship

1. Religion in India

Hinduism is the religion of most of the people who live in India. Today there are also many Hindus living in other parts of the world.
The words 'Hindu' and 'India' come from the name of the great River Indus in the part of north-west India which is now Pakistan.

The religion which became known as Hinduism has its roots among the people who lived in the Indus valley more than 4000 years ago.
No one great person founded (began) Hinduism.
Nor is there one particular holy book as in many other religions.
The religion grew from the way people lived and the way they thought of God. They passed on their beliefs to their children by teaching them stories and hymns about God. Many of these were later written down in a number of holy books (see p. 5). Some of their ancient religious customs are still in use today, such as worship around a sacred fire (see the photograph of a havan ceremony on p. 17).

India is a huge country.
The land in the north is quite different from that in the south. So is the weather.
Over the centuries, parts of India have been invaded and ruled by people from other countries with other religions.
Today India has eighteen states (regions) and many of these have their own language. It is important to know too that most of the Hindus in India live in villages. Many of them do not read or write. They may not understand their religion in the same way as more-educated city Hindus. Because of all these facts, the way Hindus live and many of their religious customs are quite different in different parts of India.
They celebrate different festivals, they build their temples differently and they worship in different ways.
There are some things that all Hindus do, but there are many things some Hindus do which other Hindus have never even heard of!

Everywhere you go in India there are signs of religion.
There are roadside shrines all over the country.
Posters advertise films of stories of gods and goddesses.
Cows wander in the streets – they are sacred animals.
In many shops and offices there is a small shrine with a lamp and incense burning.
Temples and shops give away calendars which have on them information and pictures of gods, goddesses and holy places.
Rickshaw (taxi) and truck drivers have pictures of gods and goddesses in their cabs.
Marigolds and other flowers are sold especially for offering to gods and goddesses.
Temples are visited every day and at any time of day.
Every Hindu home has a shrine for daily worship.
Hindus would say that their religion and their daily lives are not separate.
Most Hindus do not learn their religion in lessons at school or from teaching at temples. Children learn all the important things about their faith by watching what their parents and grandparents do, especially at home and at festival times.

In India 80% of the people are Hindus. On the map opposite you can find which are the other main religions in India. Sometimes you hear in the news about trouble between the different religious communities. Disputes do break out about things like land and water rights, about places of worship or about justice and power. But most of the time followers of the different religions get on very well together.
Hindus are peaceful people and have always been very tolerant of other religions. They include many holy men from other religions among their saints. At their shrines you may see pictures of Jesus, of Kabir (Muslim), of Guru Nanak (Sikh) and of the Buddha. Look at picture 7 on p. 3.

Places named in this book are marked on the map opposite.

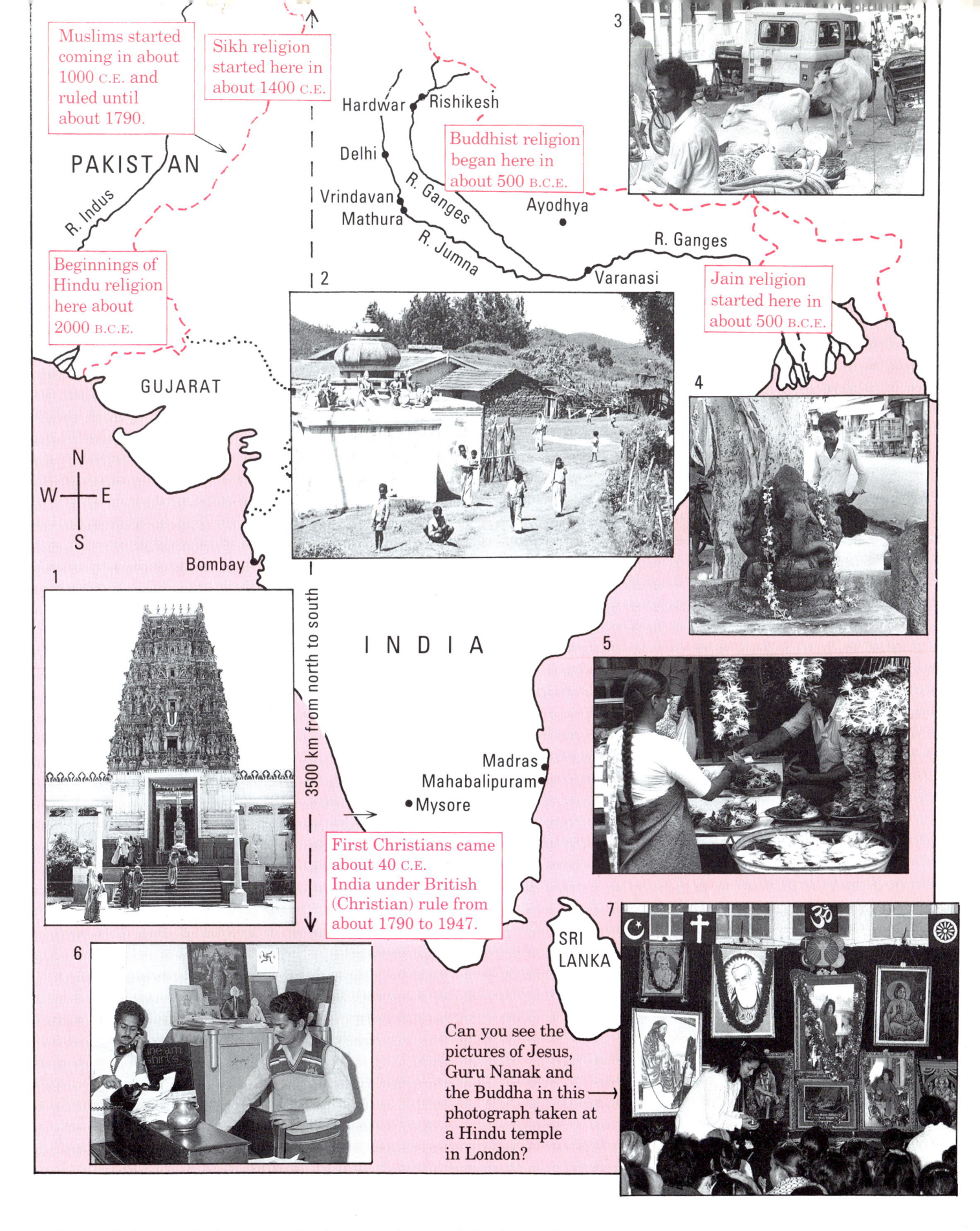

Muslims started coming in about 1000 C.E. and ruled until about 1790.

Sikh religion started here in about 1400 C.E.

Buddhist religion began here in about 500 B.C.E.

Jain religion started here in about 500 B.C.E.

Beginnings of Hindu religion here about 2000 B.C.E.

PAKISTAN
R. Indus
Hardwar Rishikesh
Delhi
Vrindavan
Mathura
R. Ganges
R. Jumna
Ayodhya
R. Ganges
Varanasi

GUJARAT

N W E S

Bombay

INDIA

3500 km from north to south

Madras
Mahabalipuram
• Mysore

First Christians came about 40 C.E. India under British (Christian) rule from about 1790 to 1947.

SRI LANKA

Can you see the pictures of Jesus, Guru Nanak and the Buddha in this photograph taken at a Hindu temple in London?

1. From which river do the names Hindu and India come? Find it on the map.
2. What is the distance from the north to the south of India?
3. Write down two or three reasons to explain why Hindu religious customs are so different in different parts of India.
4. In India 80% of people are Hindu. Name five other religions to which Indians belong. (Look on the map.)
5. Write short captions for pictures 3, 4, 5 and 6 above. (Look in the paragraph beginning 'Everywhere …' on p. 2.) Say what is happening in each picture. Where was it taken? In a town or a village?

3

2. Hindu beliefs

There are statues and pictures of many gods and goddesses in Hindu temples.
Hindus worship and pray to these images. However most Hindus would tell you that these gods and goddesses are different aspects of the Great God, the Great Soul, the Great Power which Hindus call *Brahman*. They say that people cannot see Brahman, who is above and beyond everything, and yet also within everyone and in all of nature. People can more easily pray to and express devotion to images of gods and goddesses which they can see. The character and actions of each deity show people something of what Brahman is like.
Some Hindus say they do not worship the statues, but find them helpful as a focus to worship Brahman.
Some Hindus prefer not to use images at all and use meditation and yoga when they worship (see p. 26).
There are no written rules on what a Hindu must believe.

This picture shows the holy River Ganges near where it rises in the Himalayan Mountains.
Hindus believe that God is in all forms of life and nature. From ancient times Indians have depended on the powers of nature and the weather for their livelihood as farmers. So the oldest scriptures tell of the worship of God as fire (Agni), as the sun (Savitri), as a storm (Indra). Worship around a sacred fire is still used today in the havan ceremony (see p. 17). The great River Ganges is most sacred (see p. 22). Cattle are sacred as they are providers of life – they give milk, they pull ploughs and their dung makes fuel for warmth and cooking.
In the picture below, women are mixing cow-dung with straw. It will dry in the sun. This is a common sight in India.

Here are the *Sanskrit* letters for OM or AUM. (Say it like 'home', slowly, without the 'h'.)
It is a sacred sound for Brahman. It is spoken or chanted with great reverence, often at the beginning of a prayer or hymn. 'Om shanti' is a much used prayer for peace. The symbol is seen in most Hindu homes and temples.

4

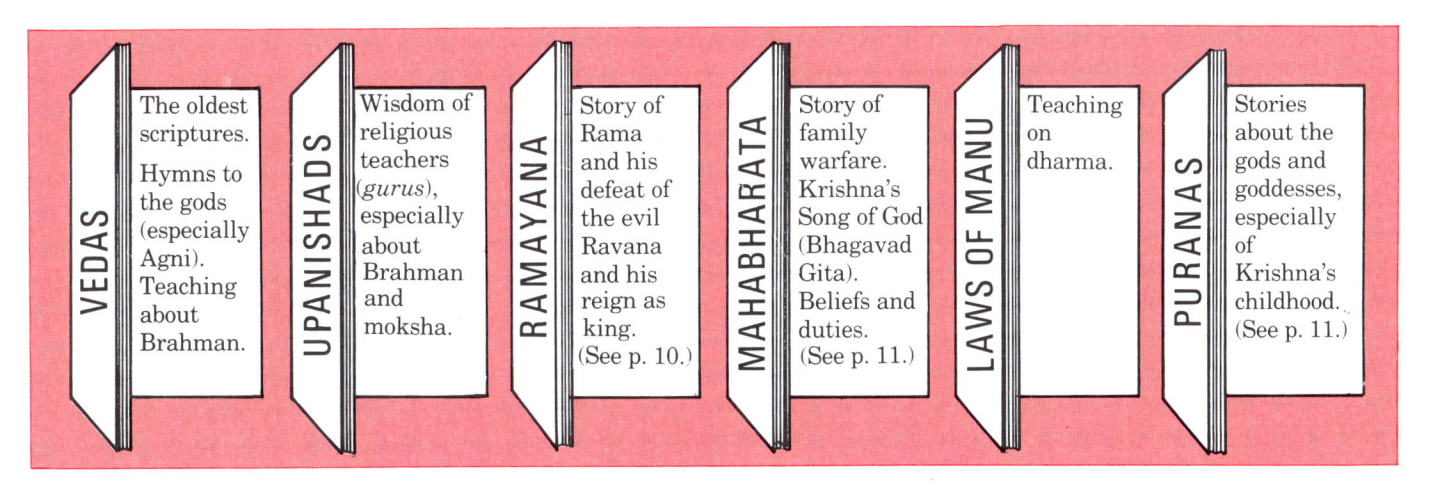

VEDAS	UPANISHADS	RAMAYANA	MAHABHARATA	LAWS OF MANU	PURANAS
The oldest scriptures. Hymns to the gods (especially Agni). Teaching about Brahman.	Wisdom of religious teachers (*gurus*), especially about Brahman and moksha.	Story of Rama and his defeat of the evil Ravana and his reign as king. (See p. 10.)	Story of family warfare. Krishna's Song of God (Bhagavad Gita). Beliefs and duties. (See p. 11.)	Teaching on dharma.	Stories about the gods and goddesses, especially of Krishna's childhood. (See p. 11.)

SAMSARA

One of the central Hindu beliefs is in *samsara* or rebirth, also called reincarnation. It means that when your body dies, your soul (*atman*) is born again into another body (it may be human or animal).

'Just as a man discards old clothes and buys new ones, the atman discards worn-out bodies and enters new ones,'

says the holy book called the Bhagavad Gita (2:22).
Each soul will have many lives on earth. In each life you should try to be better, to love God more, to work hard and to serve other people. Your actions in this life will decide what will happen to you in your next life. This idea is called *karma*. Your aim is to become so close to Brahman that when you die, your soul will not be born again but be united with Brahman. This is called *moksha*, meaning freedom from being reborn.

DHARMA

Hinduism teaches that each person has a *dharma*.
This means 'religious duties'. People's dharma depends on their family, their age, their job and their *caste* (place in society, see p. 19). For example, parents have a duty to do the best for their children. Children have a duty to show respect to their parents and to work hard at school. People with particular skills have a duty to use them for the benefit of others in the community or for their country. A person who is rich and powerful has a duty to help those who are poor and powerless. All people have the religious duty to do their work to the best of their ability and to do 'what is right'.

Above are the most important of the Hindu sacred books. They were written in the ancient Sanskrit language. Most Hindus cannot read Sanskrit, but they know many of the Sanskrit hymns and verses which are used in worship. The stories are well known. Puranikas (public story-tellers) and plays are very popular, especially at festival times. Huge crowds come to take part. Nowadays the books are translated into many other languages.

Below, a priest reads from the Puranas by the River Ganges.

1. What is the Hindu name for God?
2. Look closely at the picture on p. 4 taken in a temple in Birmingham. Write down what you can see.
3. Draw the sacred OM symbol. Look for the symbol in pictures on pages 9, 17 & 31 in this book.
4. Why are the cows regarded by Hindus as sacred? Look at the photographs with cows in on pp. 3, 13 and 16.
5. One of the central Hindu beliefs is in samsara. What does it mean?
6. What sort of actions should a person take to have a good karma?
7. (a) What does 'dharma' mean? Give on example. (b) Which holy book contains teaching on dharma?
8. Write down the names of the main Hindu holy books. What is the Ramayana about?
9. What are the people doing in the picture on this page?

3. Gods and goddesses

On these pages are some of the best-known gods and goddesses of Hinduism. Remember that Brahman is, for most Hindus, the Great Spirit, God above and beyond all the other deities. Brahman cannot be seen. There can be no pictures or statues of Brahman. Brahman is beyond shape or form.

There are three main gods: Brahma, the creator god, Vishnu, the preserver god, and Shiva, the regenerator god (who watches over death and rebirth). These days most Hindus are followers of either Shiva or Vishnu. They are great and powerful gods.

There are many other gods and goddesses. Hindus honour and respect all the deities. But most Hindus choose one god or goddess to whom they will show special devotion, particularly at home. Probably the most popular are Rama and Krishna. See chapter 4.

In the picture on the right taken in Mahabalipuram, in south India, young men are carving images of the deities out of stone. These carvings will be sent to temples all over India and even to other parts of the world.
There is a college of sculpture here where students learn the traditional ways to make statues of each of the gods and goddesses.

BRAHMA
(*Not the same as Brahman.*)
The creator god. He is often shown with four heads facing north, south, east and west. He carries a book (the holy Vedas), a string of prayer-beads, a jar and a ladle (objects used in worship). His wife is the beautiful Saraswati, goddess of music, art and learning.
In her hand is a musical instrument called a vina. They both sit on lotus flowers and usually ride on swans. Saraswati is worshipped especially on the last three days of the festival of Navaratri and on a spring day when she blesses books and school equipment.

A HINDU STORY OF CREATION
Before the world is created Vishnu sleeps on the coils of Shesha, a giant snake with a thousand heads. They float on the sea of eternity. A lotus grows from Vishnu's navel and Brahma comes out of the lotus and creates the world.

VISHNU

The preserver god. He carries a lotus, a conch shell, a mace and a discus (a magic weapon which destroys evil).
His skin is usually blue.
Vishnu has had nine avatars, which means he has come back to earth, in disguise, nine times. He comes to help when humankind is in bad trouble.
He is expected to come again. His most famous avatars are Rama and Krishna. In them Vishnu returned to earth as perfect men with powers to conquer evil (see chapter 4).

Lakshmi is Vishnu's wife. She is the goddess of wealth and good fortune. She brings prosperity when worshipped at Divali (see p. 25).
She carries a conch shell and a lotus flower and she sits or stands on a lotus plant. Gold coins fall from one hand and often there are elephants with her.

At the entrance to Malakshmi Temple in Bombay, a woman sells coconuts and lotus flowers for people to offer at the shrine inside.

You will notice that many of the deities have several heads and arms. Their extra limbs show the superhuman powers they have from God. Brahma, for example, has four heads and can therefore see all corners of the world at once. Each deity carries something in each hand. There are many stories to explain these objects and also to explain the 'vehicle' (usually an animal) on which each deity rides. Some deities are known by more than one name. Shiva is also called Shankara, Rudra or Mahesh (often depending on which part of India you are in). Others appear in different forms with different names. Shiva's wife is worshipped sometimes as the kind and gentle Parvati, sometimes as the warrior goddess Durga. Sometimes she is Kali, who comes in great anger to the world to destroy evil.

Hindus treat the statues of the deities (called *murti*) with great respect and love, often as if they were kings or queens. (Look at the picture of the crowns on p. 9.)
In temples they are 'put to bed' at night; the *arti* ceremony (see p. 13) is performed in front of them and the curtains are drawn across. In the morning they are woken (with bells) and dressed. They are adorned with jewellery and flowers. Food is offered to them and later it is shared out among the worshippers.
When a new statue is installed a special *puja* is offered.
Images in home shrines are looked after in a similar way.

On the right is a special Durga puja in a Birmingham temple. Water, milk, yoghurt, honey and ghee (melted butter) are poured over the statue to honour Durga.

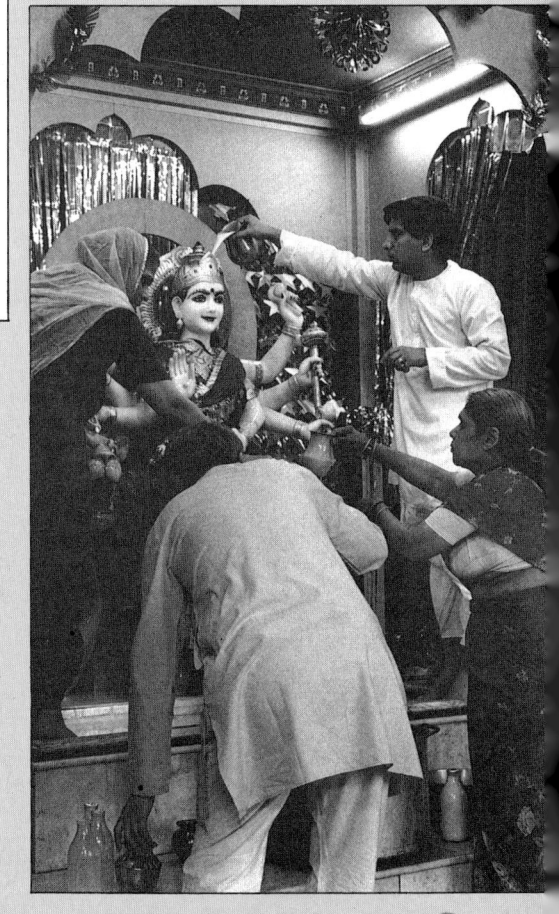

SHIVA

The regenerator god who is present at death so that new life can take its place.
There is nearly always a Shiva temple at a ghat (cremation ground, see p. 21). Here he is shown as a holy man, with long hair piled up. His skin is blue. He sits on a tiger skin holding a trident and prayer-beads. A cobra is coiled round his neck.
The River Ganges flows down from his hair (story on p. 22). His vehicle is Nandi, a bull.

Sometimes Shiva is shown as the Lord of the Dance.
He dances in a circle of fire and treads the dwarf of ignorance under his feet. The energy he uses to dance keeps the world going.
The circle of fire is time with no beginning or end.
Once a year Hindus pray and sing and fast all night in honour of Shiva as Lord of the Dance. This is called Mahashivratri, which means 'the great night of Shiva'.

The symbol of Shiva is a linga. You will see this in most temples. It is a short rounded pillar usually made of stone or marble. It represents the power to regenerate life.
Find pictures on pp. 9 and 15.

Shiva's wife has several forms. As Parvati she is beautiful and gentle.
She holds her son Ganesh the elephant god by her knee.
As Durga she is the warrior goddess. In her hands she carries deadly weapons with which she slew a buffalo demon. She rides on a tiger or a lion.

Shiva

Parvati

Ganesh

Durga

Ganesh is a favourite god. He carries an axe (to remove obstacles), a noose (used to catch wild elephants) and one of his favourite sweets.
His vehicle is a rat.
Nearly every shrine has a statue of him and prayers are usually said to him first. He is thought of as the remover of obstacles (problems) so Hindus pray especially to him before, for example, starting a new job or taking an exam.

Here is a story of how he got his elephant head:
Parvati was having a shower and asked Ganesh to guard the door and not let anyone in. Shiva returned home but Ganesh would not let him in. As Shiva had been away for some time, he did not know Ganesh (whom Parvati had created in his absence), so in his anger he cut off the boy's head. Parvati was very upset and said Shiva must restore her son's head.
Shiva said that he would give the head of the next living thing that he met to the boy. It was an elephant. And that is why Ganesh has the head of an elephant.

Before the marriage begins, the priest performs puja to Ganesh in the home of this bride.

THE GODDESS

Many Hindus see the female aspect of God as the most powerful force (shakti) in the world. They will choose a form of the Goddess for their special devotion.

She may be worshipped as Saraswati, Lakshmi, Parvati, Durga, Amba, Kali or as a less-well known local goddess. The Goddess is known by many names, sometimes simply as Devi (the Goddess). Other names are Mata, Mataji or just Ma. These all mean 'Mother'.

Saris swirl, sticks clash and drums beat as Hindus from Gujarat dance around the shrine of Mataji at this temple in London. It is the festival of Navaratri. For nine nights they sing and dance around a four-sided revolving shrine with statues of Saraswati, Durga, Amba and Kali.

These are very precious old crowns and jewels in south India, with which the gods and goddesses are decorated on festival days. Often they are paraded in the streets.

The photograph below shows statues of the most popular Hindu deities. The main gods worshipped at this temple in London are Rama and Krishna, so they are in the centre.

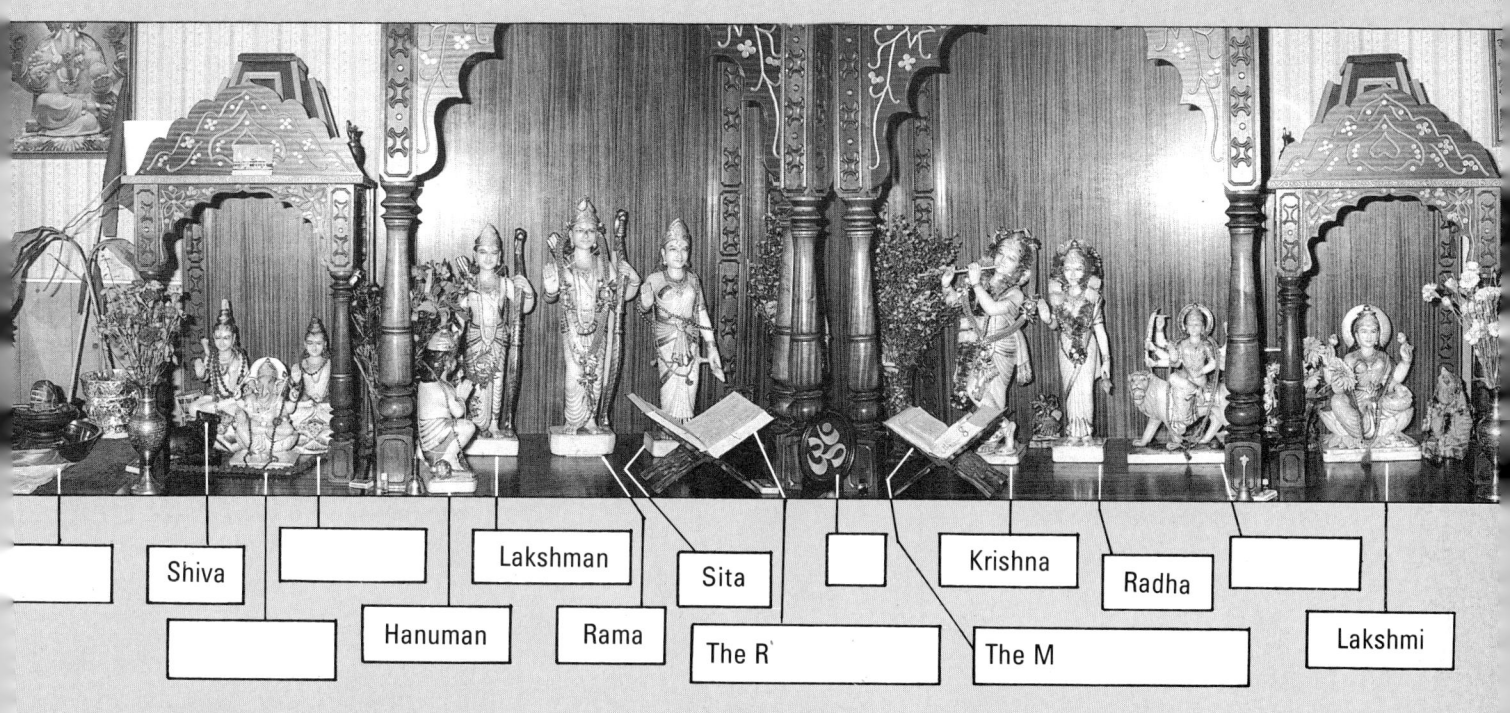

Labels: Shiva, Hanuman, Lakshman, Rama, Sita, The R, Krishna, The M, Radha, Lakshmi

1. Which are the three main gods of Hinduism?
2. Why do statues and pictures of some deities have several heads and arms?
3. What are the young men doing in the photograph on p. 6?
4. How are the murti (statues) looked after?
5. Which deity rides on each of these creatures: (a) a swan, (b) a bull, (c) a tiger (or lion), (d) a rat?
6. The lotus plant is a sacred plant like a water lily. Which deities carry or sit on a lotus?
7. The female aspect of God is very important in Hinduism. What are some of the names for the Goddess?
8. What is happening in the picture of the festival of Navaratri?
9. Draw and colour the picture of the Hindu creation story. Label with pointers Vishnu, Shesha and Brahma.
10. Copy or trace the statues and books in the photograph above and fill in the missing labels.

4. Rama and Krishna

Rama and Krishna are perhaps the most popular of all the Hindu gods. They were the seventh and eighth avatars (appearances on earth) of the great god Vishnu (see p. 7). They came to earth to save humankind from evil.

THE STORY OF RAMA

Rama was the son of the king of Ayodhya in north India. His story is told in the holy book the Ramayana.

Rama had extraordinary qualities, unlike other men. The beautiful princess Sita became his wife when he proved his strength as the only man who could lift and shoot an ancient sacred bow which had belonged to the god Shiva.

But because of a promise by his father to his stepmother, he had to go into exile for fourteen years. His beloved Sita and his dearest brother Lakshman went with him. While they were living in the forests, Sita was kidnapped by the wicked demon king Ravana. He took her far away to the island of Lanka.

Rama and Lakshman went in search of her. After many adventures and with the help of Hanuman, the monkey general, and his monkey army, the two brothers killed the ten-headed demon Ravana and rescued Sita.

At last the long exile was over and Rama and Sita and Lakshman came home. The city of Ayodhya was lit up with lanterns to welcome them.

Rama became a great, wise and just king. Hindus see in him a perfect man who defeated evil. His qualities are a model for all to follow. Rama and Sita's love for each other through great hardship is seen as an example of how marriage should be.

Below is the Lakshman Jhula hanging bridge at Rishikesh (see p. 23). It is said to be the place where Lakshman shot an arrow across the River Ganges. It made a bridge for them to cross when they returned from exile in the forests. It is now a famous place of pilgrimage. The buildings are ashrams where holy men live and pilgrims visit (see p. 26).

Many of the Hindu festivals celebrate the stories of Rama's life. There are films, plays, story-telling, puppet shows, music and dancing. Here a beautiful young dancer acts out the story of how Rama won Sita for his wife.

Hanuman, as Rama's friend and helper, is a much loved god. There are Hanuman temples all over India and the wild monkeys are sacred and never harmed.

Below, masked dancers take part in Ram Lila plays in Delhi at the festival of Dussera (see p. 25). Behind the 'monkeys' is a giant figure of the wicked Ravana. It is full of fireworks....

KRISHNA

The Mahabharata tells of the war between the Kauravas and their cousins the Pandavas. It is the longest poem in the world. It tells how the wisdom of Krishna helped the Pandavas to defeat the Kauravas at the mighty battle of Kurukshetra and so bring justice and peace to the land. The picture above shows Krishna speaking to Arjuna, a Pandava prince, while they sit in their chariot as the battle is about to begin.

This famous speech, which contains some of the most important Hindu teaching, is called the Bhagavad Gita. Many Hindu homes have a copy of this holy book.

Krishna is often worshipped as a baby. Many Hindu homes have a shrine for Lalaji or Bal-Krishna (baby Krishna). Look at the photograph below. Can you see the toys Krishna would have played with? There is a spinning-top, a dice game, a cowherd's crook, a ball and a sweet-box.

The stories of Krishna's childhood and youth are also very popular.
So as to escape murder by an evil uncle, the baby prince Krishna was smuggled away to a cowherd's family. They brought him up as their own son. He grew up in Vrindavan by the sacred River Jumna. He played the flute and was full of love and fun.
He used to get into trouble and play tricks on the milk-maids. They all loved him but his special sweetheart was Radha. Her statue often stands beside his in homes and temples. (See p. 9.)

Below is the Lakshmi Temple in Delhi, lit up for Krishna's birthday festival, called Krishna Janmashtami.

1. Look at the map on p. 3. Where are Ayodhya, Lanka (now called Sri Lanka) and Vrindavan? (North or south?)
2. What qualities in Rama do Hindus admire?
3. Why is the Lakshman Jhula bridge a famous pilgrimage place?
4. Why do you think that Hanuman is a popular god for many Hindus? Look at the pictures on p. 15.
5. What do you think will happen to the giant figure of Ravana on p. 10? Why?
6. What is the Mahabharata about? Copy or describe the chariot picture above.
7. How would you recognize Krishna in the photographs on pp. 4 and 9? (Clues: music, animal, book.)
8. Describe Krishna's childhood.
9. Draw four pictures: (a) Rama lifts and shoots Shiva's bow and arrows; (b) Sita is kidnapped by Ravana;
   (c) Hanuman and his army rescue Sita from the island of Lanka; (d) Ayodhya is lit up to welcome them home.

5. Worship

Many Hindus begin each day by washing and repeating the Gayatri Mantra. A *mantra* is a sacred verse in Sanskrit.

Much of Hindu worship is very personal. This means that each Hindu can choose how and when and which god or goddess he or she will worship. If you are a Hindu, you treat the deities as if they were honoured friends.
You call in and pay them a visit as you pass by the temple. You greet them at a shrine in someone's house. You may offer your food to them first before you eat. You want their blessing and approval for all that you do. You involve them in all of your daily life as well as the big decisions and the big occasions.

There is no one day of the week when all Hindus must go to worship or to the temple. (Although many of the deities have a 'special' day of the week. See p. 15.)
Worship can be at home, in the office, at a roadside shrine or in a temple. It can be alone or with a crowd.
Large gatherings for worship are usually for special occasions: for family events or at festival times or at places of pilgrimage.
This picture shows pilgrims gathering for the evening ceremony of arti at Hardwar on the River Ganges (see pp. 22 and 23).
In Britain there are more regular meetings for worship at weekends. (See chapter 13.)

THE GAYATRI MANTRA

In Sanskrit writing:

गायत्रि मन्त्रः

ॐ भूर् भुवः स्वः । तत् सवितुर्वरेण्यं । भर्गो देवस्य धीमहि ।
धियो यो नः प्रचोदयात् ॥   ऋक् III–62–10

This is how the Sanskrit sounds:

Om Bhur, Bhuvah, Swaha Tat Savitur Varenyam
Bhargo Devasya Dhimahi Dhiyoyonah Prachodavat.

This is what it means in English:

Oh God, Creator and Life-Giver of the Universe;
Everywhere and in all things,
We meditate on your Splendour and Divine Light
And pray for purity of mind and knowledge of the Truth.

Puja and arti are the two forms of worship used most often. They may be performed in the temple or quietly at home. Puja is when offerings of food, flowers and money are made to a god or goddess. It may be a very simple act or it can be a complicated ritual with coloured powders, rice, plants, coconuts, cotton threads, jars of ghee, water, milk and so on which only a priest will know how to conduct. (See also pp. 7 and 8.)

At the arti ceremony a flame is circled in front of the deity, with prayers and songs. Then it is handed round on a tray among the worshippers. They pass their hands over the flame, across their eyes and over their heads. They receive the blessing of the deity. Sometimes on the arti tray are symbols of the four elements:
fire (flame),
earth (flowers, incense),
air (a fan, a conch shell)
and water.

Arti at a temple in Coventry.

Special events are usually led by one or more priests (see p. 27). Most of the words would be in Sanskrit.
An important part of worship is the actions and gestures which show respect and joy and honour. Hindus often touch or kiss the steps of a shrine and the feet of a deity or a holy man. They greet the deities with the anjali greeting: hands held together, fingers pointing upwards, meaning 'honour to you'. (This is a common greeting between people too, with the word 'namaste'.) They sing hymns, they chant mantras, they clap and beat rhythms with cymbals and tambourines.
Musicians play the harmonium and tabla (drums). There may be dancing. Bells are rung and a conch shell is blown.
At the end of worship water is sprinkled over the people. Sweets, fruit and nuts that have been blessed by the deities are now called *prashad* and are shared among the people.

Learning to play the tabla and harmonium.

Because Hindus believe that God is in all forms of life and nature, worship can be of a river, a tree, an animal.
Certain places, animals and plants are sacred because they have links with a particular deity. Examples are monkeys (Hanuman), cows and peacocks (Krishna), snakes (Shiva), tulsi plants (Vishnu). Pipal trees are linked with ancestors. Hindus honour their ancestors with special acts of worship; perhaps on an anniversary (see p. 30) or when they make a pilgrimage.

Puja is offered to a cow and her new-born calf at a temple in Bombay.

1. Write down the different sorts of places where Hindus worship. Look for pictures in this book.
2. What is puja worship? What are the people doing in the puja pictures above and on pp. 7 and 8?
3. How can you tell which are the two arti photographs on this page and p. 12?
4. What sounds might you hear during Hindu worship? Draw a tabla.
5. What happens at the end of worship among a group of Hindus?
6. Why is puja being offered to a cow and her calf in the picture above?
7. Hindus use many objects and symbols in worship. Draw the arti tray and label the objects.
8. Make a Hindu greetings card (perhaps for one of the festivals – see chapter 11). Copy onto (or into) it the sacred Gayatri Mantra in Sanskrit. Talk about the English translation with a friend.

6. Temples

A temple (or *mandir*) is a building which houses one or more of the gods and goddesses. Statues of the deities (called murti) live in the temple. Hindus visit the temple to offer to them gifts, and prayers and devotion. Each temple has a main god or goddess who is especially honoured.

Sometimes temples are built where an event in the life of one of the deities or Hindu saints took place. Many of these temples have become pilgrimage centres (see p. 22). Temples are often built near a river. Water washes and makes a person pure and holy. It is the source of life, especially in a hot country.

The two women below are painting sacred patterns (called rangoli) with coloured rice powders in the courtyard of a temple in Madras.

Above is one of the vast ancient temples in south India. The great gateway is a pyramid of thousands of stone carvings of the deities.

Inside is a huge courtyard. There are many shrines for different gods and goddesses with beautiful statues and carvings. Many are brightly painted. A priest takes gifts of flowers, food or money from the worshippers and offers them to the deities (look at the picture below right). The worshippers receive some food back as prashad (see p. 13). The priest marks their foreheads with ash or a spot of red paste (called a tilak).

A shrine in the centre of the temple contains the statue of the main god or goddess. It is a small dark room dimly lit by oil-lamps. Worshippers file past for a glimpse of the deity (*darshan*). Some temples do not allow non-Hindus into this most holy part of the temple. Cameras are forbidden.

Here are three photographs taken at a village temple. It is built around some hot springs. People bathe in the healing waters before they worship. Hanuman, the monkey god (see p. 10), is the main god worshipped here. Wild monkeys often come down from the hillside. They are never harmed, they are sacred animals.

It is Hanuman's special day of the week. The villagers gather in the evening to bring gifts of food, flowers and money and to receive darshan (sight of him) – being in his presence will bring them blessings. The shrine is in the middle of the picture, by the tree. It is a sacred pipal tree. From the tree trunk hang pieces of cloth and threads and messages. These are special requests to the deities to heal someone who is ill or to keep away evil spirits or to bring a good harvest or a safe childbirth. There is a pipal tree at most temples in India. The photograph above is a close-up of the shrine. You can see the image of Hanuman, which is painted shiny silver and orange.

When people come to a temple they take off their shoes.
They enter and wash (or bathe if there is a pool).
As they approach the main deity they may ring a hanging bell and then kneel and bow their head to the ground.
They may spend a few minutes praying before each of the deities and make offerings to one or more of them. They may pour some water or milk over the Shiva linga (see p. 8).
Look at the photograph on the right, taken in London.
The worshipper may now leave or sit quietly in front of one of the statues or perhaps chat to a friend. There are no chairs in a temple. People sit on the ground. In some temples men sit on one side and women and children on the other. The priest gives prashad to each person as they leave. Every temple has one or more priests (see p. 27).

1. What is a Hindu temple for?
2. What are the two women doing in the left-hand small picture on p. 14?
3. What is the priest doing in the right-hand small picture on p. 14? What will he do next?
4. What does 'darshan' mean?
5. Write down what you know about Hanuman. (See also p. 10.)
6. Describe what you can see in the three photographs at the top of this page.
7. What is special about the pipal tree?
8. What do Hindus do when they enter a temple? Write your answer or make drawings.
9. Describe what the woman in the photograph above is doing. Why is there a bull beside the linga? (Clue: see p. 8.)
10. Describe what you can see in the big photograph on p. 14 and on the cover of this book. Draw a picture.

7. At home

Shrine labels:
- OM or AUM (sacred sound for God)
- Swastika, symbol for God's blessings
- Photo of temple at Kedarnath (see p. 23)
- Mataji with trident (called 'trishul' – a weapon to fight against evil)
- Krishna (has black skin and plays the flute)
- Crocodile – Mataji sometimes rides on a crocodile
- Picture of Hanuman
- Box with Divali coins in it, a flower and silver sandals (symbol for Mataji's holy footsteps)
- Peacock feathers
- Siddhul vinayak – coconut (a symbol for Ganesh)
- The Bhagavad Gita
- Book of hymns and prayers
- Copper jar with water from the River Ganges sealed in it
- Prayer-beads, called 'mala' (made from seeds of tulsi plants)
- Cobra (sacred to Shiva)
- Divas (lights)

This is the doorway of a Hindu house in Varanasi.
The cows live behind the house in a courtyard.
Many Hindu homes have pictures painted around the front door. Can you see the picture of Hanuman?
There are other signs and symbols to keep away evil spirits and bring blessings of the deities to the house. Sometimes they are painted on the doorstep.
The swastika is an ancient Hindu symbol which stands for good fortune and God's blessing.

People usually take off their shoes when they enter a house in India.

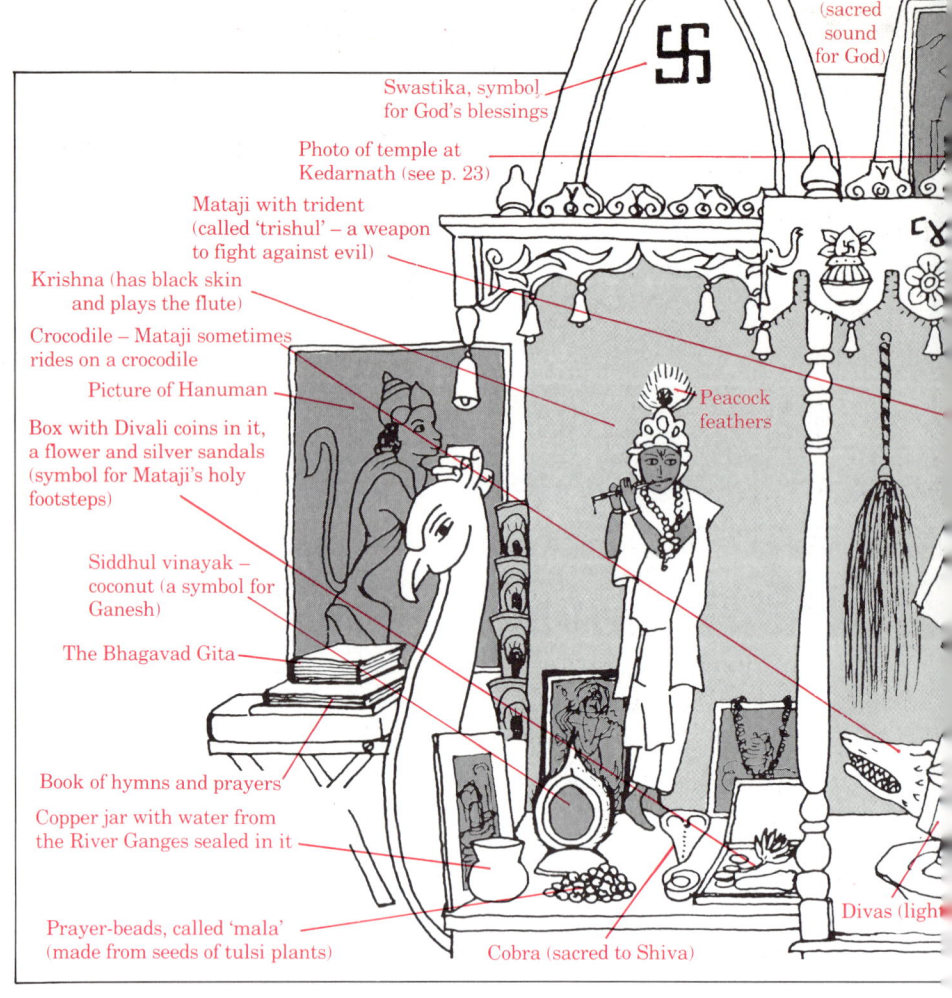

Inside nearly every Hindu home is a shrine (mandir) with pictures or statues of one or more gods and goddesses.
Some homes have enough space to set aside a small room for their shrine, as the photograph above left shows.
The drawing shows the shrine in detail. Look carefully at it. From time to time the family wash the statues and change their clothes and jewellery. They have collected sacred objects from the holy places they have visited in India.
The mother offers puja most mornings after her husband has gone to work and the children are at school. In the evening the family sometimes light the *divas* (lamps) and say the arti prayers together. The home shrine is the centre point of many family events and celebrations. There is a real feeling that the god or goddess is present in the house with the family.

Labels on the drawing (left):
- Sri, a title of respect and honour
- Jai Khodiarma, one of the names for Mataji
- Whisks, used to fan royalty or honoured people in hot weather (see p. 26)
- Bells
- Trident
- Leaves pressed from a bilipatra tree (sacred to Shiva)
- Picture of Durga
- Peacocks – sacred birds (the national bird of India)
- Photo of husband's parents
- Photo of Guru Venkateshwa
- Dish with Ganesh, a sacred thread, a cobra and two betel nuts (symbols for Ganesh's wives)
- Bell
- Incense holder in the shape of OM
- Bells and gong to attract the attention of the deity

The photograph below shows a havan (sacred fire) ceremony in Coventry.
A young family is moving house today. The day begins with a special blessing of the new house. About forty members of the family gather for the havan. A sacred fire is burned and Agni, the god of fire, is worshipped.
The priest (in the centre of the picture) brings a metal container filled with wood. In the middle of the living room the fire is lit and ghee and incense and rice are sprinkled in. Prayers and hymns are chanted to bless and purify the new home. This is followed by a meal and a lot of family chatter. Children learn about their religion by watching closely everything that happens.

Look at the picture on the left. In this house there is a simple shrine in the kitchen.
The shrine should be kept clean and pure so the kitchen is a good place for it.
Also the family like to offer their food to the deity for blessing before they eat.
Most Hindus do not eat meat. They are vegetarian. They do not like to harm animals. Rice, vegetables, dried beans and lentils are usually cooked with tasty spices and chilli peppers.

1. There are often religious pictures and symbols painted at the entrance to a Hindu home. Why?
2. Write a sentence to describe each of the home shrines on p. 16.
3. Why is the kitchen a good place for a shrine? Look at the Bal-Krishna shrine on p. 11.
4. What do you know about food eaten by Hindus?
5. What is happening in the photograph above?
6. Write a list of six to ten questions about the drawing above. Swap them with a friend and try to answer each other's questions (talking, not writing).
7. Copy or get a photocopy of the drawing above and colour it.

8. Hindu families

Among Indians the family is not just mother, father and children. The family means grandparents, uncles, aunts and cousins. Most often they live together or nearby.
A bride usually goes to live with her husband's parents after the wedding and she becomes part of his family. The parents' house is often home for several of their sons with their wives and children. Sometimes the sons' families take turns to live with their parents. Children often call their cousins 'brother' or 'sister'.
Money is shared. Brothers, fathers and uncles help each other in business.
Older people are respected and valued and usually help to bring up their grandchildren. There are no such places as 'Homes for Old People' in India.
Honour is also shared, which means that every member of the family must behave well. If one member of the family does something bad, it will bring disgrace to the whole family.

Many of the family traditions described here and in chapter 9 are the social custom among most Indians, whatever their religion.

In this photograph a Hindu grandmother is telling her grandson about all the objects in the shrine at a friend's house.

Above is a picture taken at Raksha Bandhan. This is a popular Hindu festival when brothers and sisters show their love for each other. Sisters tie a rakhi (bracelet) round their brothers' wrists. Brothers give their sisters presents.
The girl is tying a rakhi of silvery threads onto her brother. He is giving her some money. On the tray is a pile of rakhis – remember cousins count as brothers too!
And mothers and aunts also give rakhis to their brothers. Imagine the amount of visiting that goes on today!
Also on the tray are Indian sweets to eat and rice and red paste to make the tilak mark on each other's foreheads. This shows that it is a religious occasion, as are most family events.

CASTE

Hindu families belong in groups called varnas. There are four varnas: Brahmin, Kshatrya, Vaisha and Shudra. Within these groups are hundreds more smaller groups called castes.

A system of organizing society was worked out thousands of years ago in India like this:

> The Brahmins were the **thinkers** (priests, teachers, lawyers).
> The Kshatryas were the **protectors** (rulers, warriors).
> The Vaishas were the **businessmen** (traders, craftsmen, peasant farmers).
> The Shudras were the **labourers** who worked on the land and served the other three groups.

This caste system is, in many ways, still very strong among Hindus today. Outside these groups are the 'Untouchables'. Many of these people still do the jobs that nobody else wants to do.

A child is born into the same caste as its parents.
A Hindu cannot change caste and should marry someone from the same caste. Usually and especially in the villages, sons learn the same jobs as their fathers. Occupations belong to particular castes. Everybody knows where they fit in and how they should behave according to their caste (this is part of dharma – see p. 5). Hindus believe that their actions in this life may affect which caste they are born into in their next life when they die (this is part of karma – see p. 5).

Along with caste, the idea of purity is very important to most Hindus. Before worship they always bathe or wash. They want their bodies and their minds to be pure. Particular things are considered 'polluting' or impure. Anything that comes out of the body, such as sweat or spit, is polluting. A dead body is very polluting. Usually the lower castes wash the (sweaty) clothes, clean toilets and tan the skins (of dead animals) for leather. Because they do these kinds of job, they are considered impure, untouchable and higher-caste Hindus do not mix with them. These customs and rules are kept more strictly in some places than in others.

These days many Indians think caste divisions are unjust and wrong so conditions are beginning to change. Laws have been passed so that members of all the lower castes have more opportunities. For example, all castes are now allowed by law to go into temples and to go to universities.

Above: Untouchables sweep the streets in India.

Below: Men from the top three castes may wear a 'sacred thread'. A twisted cotton thread is worn across the left shoulder. It may be changed once a year. The ceremony often takes place beside water, as the picture shows. See also p. 21.

---

1. 'Joint' or 'extended' are words often used to describe Indian families. Why do you think this is?
2. Indian families usually help and support each other. What sorts of things do they share?
3. (a) What is happening in the Raksha Bandhan photograph? (b) How can you tell it is a religious occasion?
4. Which of the four varnas would you expect these people to belong to: (a) a priest, (b) a shopkeeper, (c) a cowherd, (d) a soldier?
5. Why do the 'Untouchables' have this name? What job is the Untouchable doing in the picture on this page?
6. Fill in the missing words: 'A Hindu cannot _____ caste and should marry someone from the _____ caste.'
7. (a) Why do Hindus wash before they worship? (b) What sorts of things do Hindus consider 'polluting'?
8. Who are the men in the picture above? Explain why they are there.

9. Samskara

Samskara is the word used for religious rituals which mark important times in a Hindu's life. With large families living together (see p. 18), there are always special events to be celebrated.

Friends and relatives gather for a religious ceremony, which usually takes place in the home. There are many more than those described here and customs differ in different places and among different castes.

Above: A Hindu wedding ceremony.

The bridegroom arrives for his wedding garlanded with flowers. In villages, he may come riding on a horse, as in the picture below. There are two weddings in this village today!

MARRIAGE

A Hindu marriage is nearly always a joining of two families.

Parents look for suitable partners for their sons and daughters. Sometimes the bride and groom do not meet until the day of their wedding. More often these days, the young couple spend time together beforehand to see if they like each other.

Usually there are months of preparations and exchanging of gifts between the two families.

The wedding celebrations generally take place in the bride's village or at her home. They may last for several days. Usually the bride wears a beautiful red and gold sari and gold jewellery. Her sisters and friends may have painted patterns on her hands and feet with henna (a red paste). A priest leads the long ceremony of prayers, mantras and offerings. The marriage is sealed when the couple walk seven steps together around the sacred fire.

There follows a great feast. Most often the couple go to live with the husband's family. A wife usually returns to her own parents' home for a few weeks when she has her first baby. Divorce is very unusual among Hindus.

Above is a horoscope.

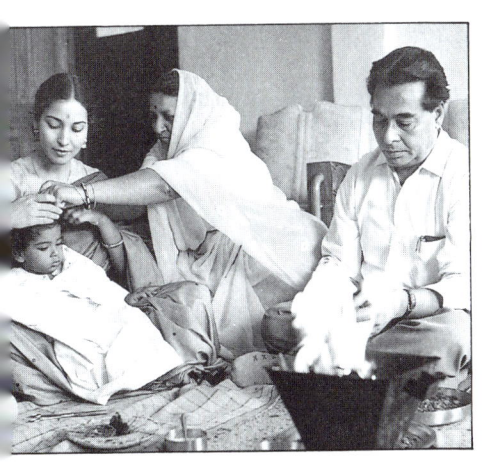

CHILDREN

A baby is given its name ten or twelve days after it is born. A priest may visit the home for this ceremony.
Later the child may be taken to the temple for a blessing or darshan (sight of the deity).
The child's horoscope is prepared soon after birth. It is a chart showing the positions of the stars and planets at the time of the baby's birth. Most Hindus believe that this affects the future of the child.
Important dates like weddings or long journeys should be planned according to a person's horoscope, in order to bring blessings and good luck and to ward off danger and evil spirits. (See p. 27.)

The picture on the left shows a mundan ceremony, when a boy's hair is cut for the first time. His head will be completely shaved. His grandfather reads the holy scriptures in front of the sacred fire.

Men and boys over seven who belong to the top three castes may wear a 'sacred thread'. At a solemn ceremony, they promise to study the holy books and to obey the advice and teaching of their guru (who may be the local priest). They receive a long loop of twisted cotton threads which is worn over the left shoulder. See also p. 19.

DEATH

When a Hindu dies, the body is wrapped in a white cloth. It is taken to the cremation ground (if it is by a river it is called a burning ghat).
The body is burned on a pyre (pile of wood). Look at the picture above.
Hindus believe that as the body burns, the soul (atman) escapes and returns to earth to be born again into a new body. This is called reincarnation (see p. 5).
Later the relatives collect the ashes and if possible they will be scattered in a nearby river. Many families try to take the ashes to the holy River Ganges (see p. 22).
Each year on the anniversary of the death, the family say shraddha prayers. There are also special weeks during the year when the dead are remembered. On p. 30 is a photograph of a shraddha ceremony in Coventry.

1. Write down three of the samskaras pictured on these two pages.
2. Where is it usual for a newly married couple to live?
3. (a) What is a horoscope? (b) Why is a horoscope important to most Hindus?
   Do you ever read your 'stars' in a magazine or newspaper? If you do, why do you?
4. What is a mundan ceremony?
5. Who wears a sacred thread? Find pictures on pp. 14, 19 and 27 of sacred threads being worn.
6. What do Hindus believe happens to a person's soul after death?
7. Draw a bride's feet painted with patterns for her wedding. (Look right.)
8. Imagine you were a guest at one of the weddings shown on p. 20. Describe what you saw and heard. In what ways was it different from a wedding in your family?

10. Pilgrimage

Pilgrimage (journey to a holy place) is an important part of the Hindu religion.
Hindus believe that the spirit of Brahman is everywhere (see p. 4). But some places are especially holy.
Pilgrimage centres usually have links with a god or goddess, or a Hindu saint or guru. Hindus want most to go to the places linked to the particular deity they worship. For example, followers of Krishna most want to go to Vrindavan and Mathura, the places where Krishna lived. Many pilgrimage places are by a river or by the sea.

Often pilgrims travel with members of their family (including grandparents and babies) or in a group from their village or their caste. They may travel only a short distance or thousands of kilometres. The harder the journey the more it shows the pilgrim's devotion to God. So many pilgrims choose to walk at least the last few kilometres to the shrine.

In some places, melas (big gatherings) are held at certain times of the year. There are huge crowds of pilgrims as in the picture above, taken at Hardwar by the River Ganges.

There are many reasons why Hindus go on a pilgrimage. First, it is a religious duty (dharma) and an act of devotion to God. Then there is the joy of being in the presence of a much loved god or goddess (darshan) and of being with other pilgrims. Many believe it will add to their good deeds (karma) and bring them nearer to moksha (freedom from rebirth). Some believe that darshan of the deity will cure them of an illness. Some come to fulfil a vow (promise), as a thank you to God because they had a good harvest or passed an exam, for example. Some come to make up for a bad deed. Some come to offer puja for a relative who has died. Many pilgrims take home small jars of river water and other holy objects such as you can see in the drawing on p. 16. Some make a video to share with friends and family at home.
So a pilgrimage is a time to concentrate completely on God and to share your faith with others. You come home strengthened in your faith and with many memories of a great religious experience.

The River Ganges is a goddess to most Hindus. The story goes that the River was born from the feet of Vishnu and guided down to earth by the holy man Bhagirath. But the flow of the river was so powerful that it was going to destroy the earth until Shiva broke its fall with his head and it flowed gently down through his hair.

The page opposite shows pilgrims at different places by the River Ganges. It rises high up in the Himalayan Mountains. There are four peaks with holy shrines near the top, which thousands of pilgrims visit each year.

HIMALAYAS   LAND OF THE GODS

JUMNOTRI Where the River Jumna rises

GANGOTRI Where the River Ganges rises

KEDARNATH Temple to Shiva

BADRINATH Temple to Vishnu

Journey's end: the temple at Kedarnath, one of the twelve great Shiva temples in India.

RISHIKESH (picture on p. 10) It is 280 km from here to the mountain top, up a narrow twisty road with the danger of landslides.

HARDWAR (pictures on pp. 12 and 22)

The last 15 km to the shrine at Kedarnath can be reached only on foot up a steep track. Elderly and sick people ride on mules.

Pilgrims have washed their saris in the river. They will spend the night sleeping under this tree.

This young couple were married three weeks ago. They have travelled 1400 km by train from Bombay. This is a very special moment when they stand in the holy water for the first time and offer Ganges puja.

VRINDAVAN Where Krishna grew up

MATHURA The birthplace of Krishna

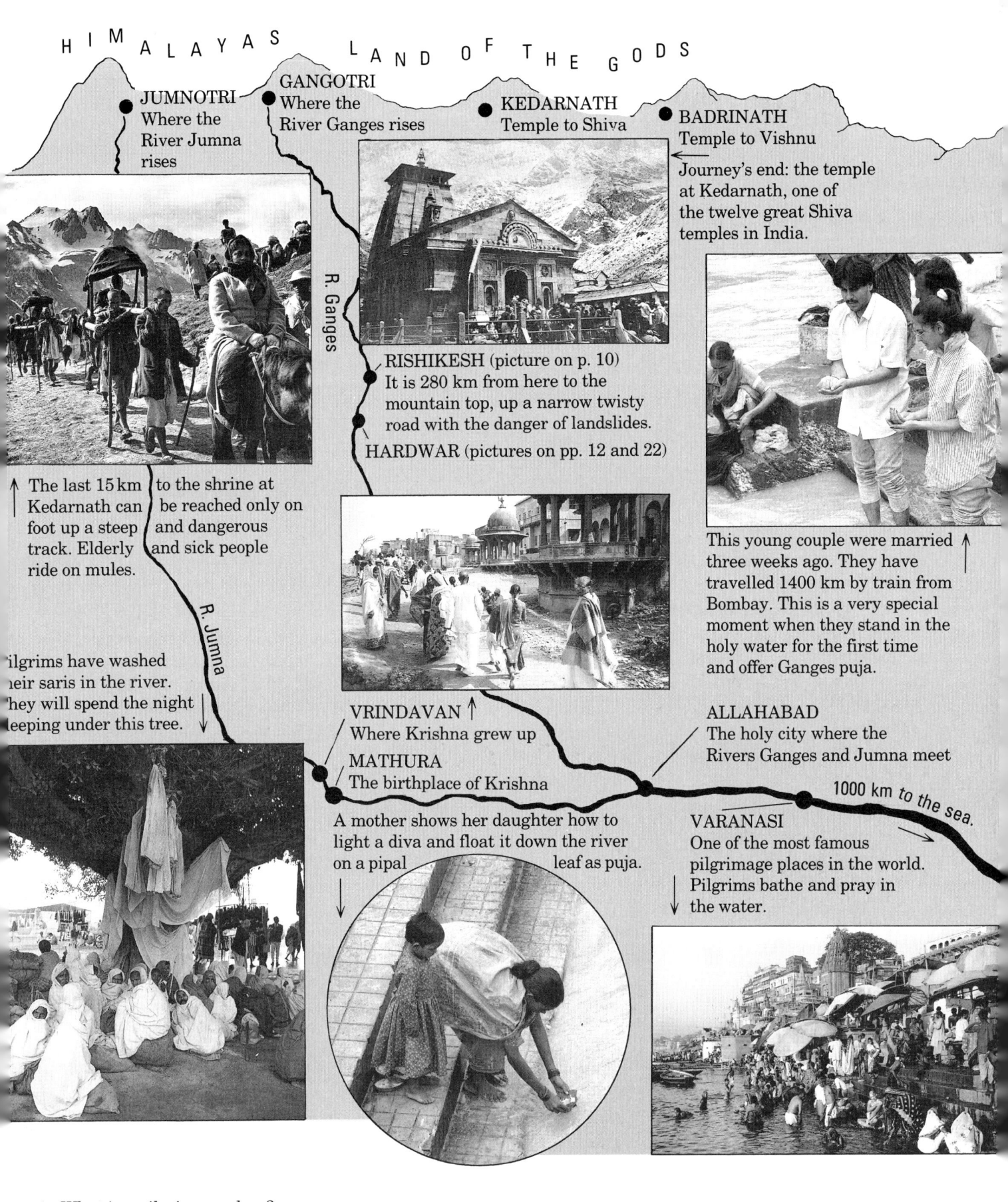

ALLAHABAD The holy city where the Rivers Ganges and Jumna meet

1000 km to the sea.

A mother shows her daughter how to light a diva and float it down the river on a pipal leaf as puja.

VARANASI One of the most famous pilgrimage places in the world. Pilgrims bathe and pray in the water.

1. What is a pilgrimage place?
2. Why are Vrindavan and Mathura famous pilgrimage places? See also p. 11.
3. Why do pilgrims often choose to walk the last few kilometres of their pilgrimage?
4. Why do Hindus go on pilgrimages? Write down two or three possible reasons.
5. Look at the drawing on pp. 16 and 17. Which objects might have come from pilgrimage places?
6. Why do you think that the Himalayan Mountains are known as the 'Land of the Gods'? Look at the picture on p. 4.
7. Draw a big picture of the story of how the River Ganges came to earth. Look at the picture of Shiva on p. 8.
8. Imagine you are one of the elderly people riding on a mule in the top left picture above. You have come all the way from England and soon you will reach the temple at Kedarnath. Write a paragraph about what you are thinking.

11. Festivals

Hindu festivals celebrate events in the lives of the gods and goddesses, or seasons like harvest and new year. Often statues of deities are carried through the streets in a joyful procession. There is music, singing and dancing. Crowds may gather for plays and story-telling about the lives of the deities. There are presents and new clothes and special sweets and food.

The best-known festivals are marked on this diagram. Divali, Holi and Navaratri are celebrated by Hindus everywhere (though in different ways). Other festivals are celebrated by Hindus in some places but not others.

This is a festival in Sri Lanka in honour of Skanda, Shiva's son. A decorated statue of Skanda is pulled along the road. Skanda (also called Murugan) is a popular god in south India, but not often worshipped in north India.

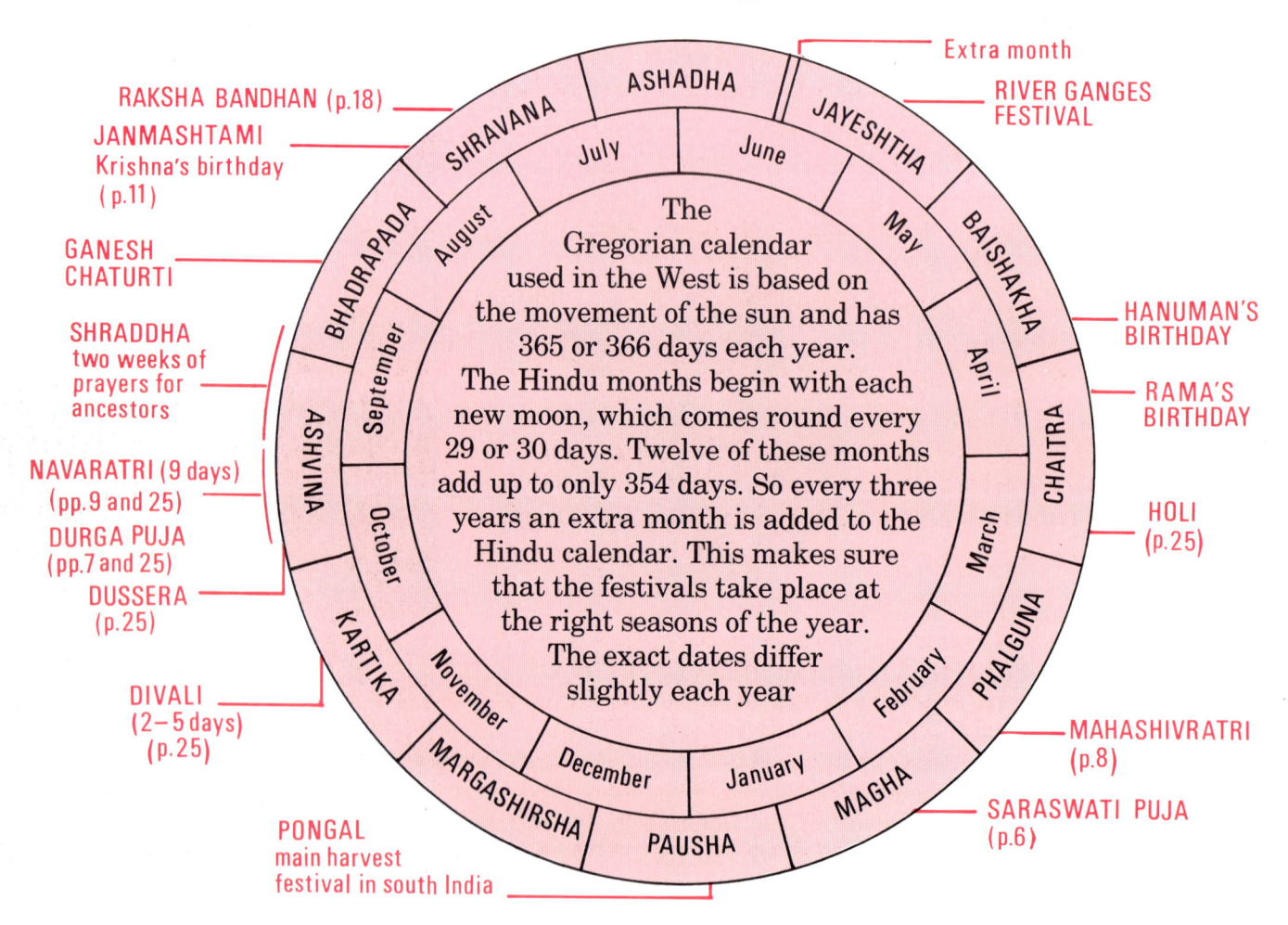

- RAKSHA BANDHAN (p.18)
- JANMASHTAMI Krishna's birthday (p.11)
- GANESH CHATURTI
- SHRADDHA two weeks of prayers for ancestors
- NAVARATRI (9 days) (pp.9 and 25)
- DURGA PUJA (pp.7 and 25)
- DUSSERA (p.25)
- DIVALI (2–5 days) (p.25)
- PONGAL main harvest festival in south India
- SARASWATI PUJA (p.6)
- MAHASHIVRATRI (p.8)
- HOLI (p.25)
- RAMA'S BIRTHDAY
- HANUMAN'S BIRTHDAY
- RIVER GANGES FESTIVAL
- Extra month

Months: ASHADHA (June), SHRAVANA (July), BHADRAPADA (August), ASHVINA (September), KARTIKA (October), MARGASHIRSHA (November), PAUSHA (December), MAGHA (January), PHALGUNA (February), CHAITRA (March), BAISHAKHA (April), JAYESHTHA (May)

The Gregorian calendar used in the West is based on the movement of the sun and has 365 or 366 days each year. The Hindu months begin with each new moon, which comes round every 29 or 30 days. Twelve of these months add up to only 354 days. So every three years an extra month is added to the Hindu calendar. This makes sure that the festivals take place at the right seasons of the year. The exact dates differ slightly each year

DIVALI is the 'festival of lights'. Look at the picture below left. In homes and temples all over India, rows of divas (lights) are lit to welcome home Rama and Sita after their defeat of Ravana (see p. 10). Divali is also the festival for Lakshmi, the goddess of wealth. Hindus light up their homes in the hope that Lakshmi will bring them good fortune. They perform special pujas to Lakshmi with coins.

In many parts of India, Divali marks the beginning of a new year and new good intentions: debts may be settled, businesses open new account books (look at the picture below right), husbands and wives may renew their marriage promises. Stories of Krishna and Rama are told – stories of good defeating evil and light overcoming darkness.

A huge silver drum is fixed onto the elephant before a Dussera procession in Mysore.

HOLI is a spring harvest festival (in north and central India there may be three harvests each year). Holi is a festival of fire and fun! Stories of Krishna and his love for Radha and of his fun and games with the milkmaids (see p. 11) are acted out today. People play tricks and squirt each other with coloured water. Yes, grown-ups too! Look at the middle picture on the right. There is music and dancing and a huge bonfire for the story of Prahlad and Holika, another story of good defeating evil.

Hindus and Sikhs enjoy themselves at Holi.

NAVARATRI lasts for nine days and is followed on the tenth day by **DUSSERA**. In north India especially, it is a festival for Rama and Sita (see p. 10). For Hindus from Gujarat, it is a time for worshipping the Goddess (see p. 9). In West Bengal, the festival is called Durga Puja. It celebrates the victory of the goddess Durga over the buffalo demon. Huge statues, like the one in the picture on the right, are carried through the streets and sunk in a river or the sea (remember water is purifying).

1. What is happening in the festival procession in the photograph on p. 24?
2. Which festivals are celebrated in the month of Shravana?
3. In which month (Hindu and western names) is Rama's birthday celebrated?
4. Why are lights such an important part of the festival of Divali?
5. What can you see in the two Divali pictures above?
6. Copy and write about one of the pictures on the right side of this page.
7. Look at the picture on p. 9. How is Navaratri being celebrated?
8. Hindu festivals are very colourful. Choose one of the festivals and design a poster for it with information and pictures.

12. Holy men

SANYASIS

The man on the left is a sanyasi, a holy man. You see sanyasis wandering all over India. 'Sanyasa' means 'to give up'. He has given up all contact with his family and all his possessions. He has only a small bundle, a begging-bowl and a stick. He wears a simple cloth and some prayer-beads. He wanders from place to place. He is given food and treated with great respect. He lives a life of meditation and prayer. He seeks moksha: he wants to become so close to God that when he dies he will not be reborn (see p. 5).

As they get older and become grandparents, many Hindus pass on most of their money and possessions to their children. They lead a simple life and spend more time on God and spiritual matters. Some men become sanyasis.

GURUS

This is another kind of holy man. 'Guru' means 'teacher' (usually of religion). In many homes and temples a picture of a guru is kept on the shrine. The family or members of the temple follow his teachings and look on him with great respect. He may be a rishi (saint) who lived many years ago or he may be a guru who lives in India today.

When a guru becomes well known for his wisdom and his teaching, he may start an ashram. This is a place where gurus and their followers live and work together. They lead a simple life based on meditation and helping other people. Hindus (and others) may stay a few days or a few months to seek peace and spiritual guidance. There is a picture on p. 10.

Some gurus are regarded almost as a god. The well-known guru in the middle picture is being carried through the street at a festival. It is an honour for his followers to carry him, to hold the canopy over his head and to fan him with the whisk.

Satya Sai Baba (bottom picture) has many thousands of followers all over the world who talk of his miracles and his teaching about right living, truth, peace, love and non-violence. They try to visit his ashram in south India. To be in his presence will bring great blessings.

MEDITATION/YOGA

Meditation is a way of praying and emptying the mind of worldly thoughts. The Hindu form of meditation, called yoga, began thousands of years ago. It is practised by many Hindus, especially sanyasis and gurus. It involves being still for a long time in different positions and concentrating deeply on God. Yoga classes in Britain usually teach exercises to help you relax, based on the Hindu yoga positions.

PRIESTS

Priests come from the Brahmin caste. (Although the 'Untouchables' – see p. 19 – may have their own priests.)
A temple priest (pujari) looks after the temple and the shrines and keeps them clean. He washes and dresses the statues of the deities. He prepares the trays for puja and arti and other special events. He receives the gifts of the worshippers and offers them to the deities. A temple priest does not have to be very learned. But he must know exactly how to perform all the religious rituals. He may live at the temple. He is paid from the money given to the temple by the worshippers.
Large temples may have many priests.
Sons of priests become priests too. Look at the picture on the right. This priest at a temple in London has begun training his son from a young age. (The elderly man is carrying a diva.)

There are also family priests. Each family may have a particular priest or guru who will perform rituals for their family events such as a wedding or naming a baby or blessing a house. He will also advise the family on spiritual and practical matters. The family pay him for these services.
Both kinds of priest may conduct rituals in the temple or in the home.

ASTROLOGY

Many priests are also astrologers. They are experts in the movement of the sun, moon, stars and planets. They consult books called almanacs and cast people's horoscopes (see p. 21) and advise on 'auspicious times'. The man in the picture on the right is consulting the priest at his local temple. Most Hindus believe that important events like a wedding, opening a new shop, planting crops or going on a pilgrimage will be blessed if they choose the right day according to their horoscope.

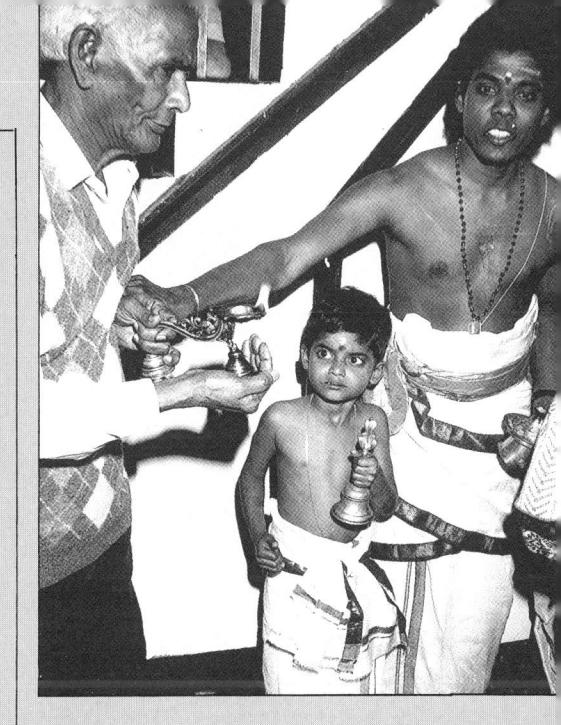

This chapter is called 'Holy men'. Of course Hindu women are holy too! In the home the women do most of the worship and in some temples women take a leading part. But there are no women priests and very few well-known women gurus. These women in Coventry (on the left) meet every week to sing hymns together.

1. (a) Look at the picture of the sanyasi. What possessions does he have? (b) Why do some men become sanyasis?
2. In the middle picture on p. 26, how is the guru being shown honour and respect? (See also the picture on p. 24.)
3. What is an ashram?
4. Satya Sai Baba has many followers who live in England. Why do they want to visit his ashram in south India?
5. What does 'meditation' mean? Find and copy some pictures of yoga positions.
6. What kind of samskaras and service will a family priest perform? (Chapter 9 will help you.)
7. Look at the picture of the man with the priest/astrologer. What do you think they might be saying to each other?
8. With a friend, imagine you are the pujari (temple priest) and his son in the picture above. You are preparing the temple and the statues for a special puja today. Write a conversation which includes questions and answers about what you are doing. Look also at chapters 5 and 6.

13. Hindus in Britain

In Britain there about 800 000 people whose families came originally from India.
Of those, about 360 000 may be Hindu. The others are mostly Sikhs and Muslims. Some are Christians.
There are Hindus living in all the large cities in Britain. About three-quarters of them come from Gujarat in India.

WHY HAVE HINDUS COME TO BRITAIN?

Britain and India have had close links for 400 years, ever since British (and other European) explorers found that India had valuable products like diamonds, ivory, pepper and spices, tiger skins and, later, tea and cotton. They set up trade companies and made themselves rulers. The Indians worked for them.

During this century, the Indians struggled to become independent of foreign rulers and govern themselves. The British left India at last in 1947. The Indians who were Muslims wanted their own separate country. So the north-west part of India (where most Muslims lived) was divided off and became Pakistan. A smaller part of north-east India was made East Pakistan and later became Bangladesh.
As members of the British Commonwealth and holders of British passports, Indians were free to come to Britain.

Above are Hindus at worship in Birmingham.

After the Second World War, in the 1950s, there were not enough people to do certain jobs in Britain. The British Government invited people in India and Pakistan and the Caribbean to come and work in the factories and hospitals and on the buses and trains. Most people in India are very poor compared to those in Western countries. So many came. They hoped to have a better standard of living and earn enough money to help their families in India.
Many came from small villages and found city life in Britain very different.

You may also meet Hindus who have come from Africa. Their families had been settled in Africa for seventy years or so. The British took many skilled Indians over to help build the railways in East Africa. At that time the British also ruled much of Africa. When the East Africans became independent of British rule, they did not want the Indians in their countries. In 1972 all the Indians living in Uganda were forced to leave. The other East African countries made it difficult for Indians to stay. Many came to Britain as refugees.

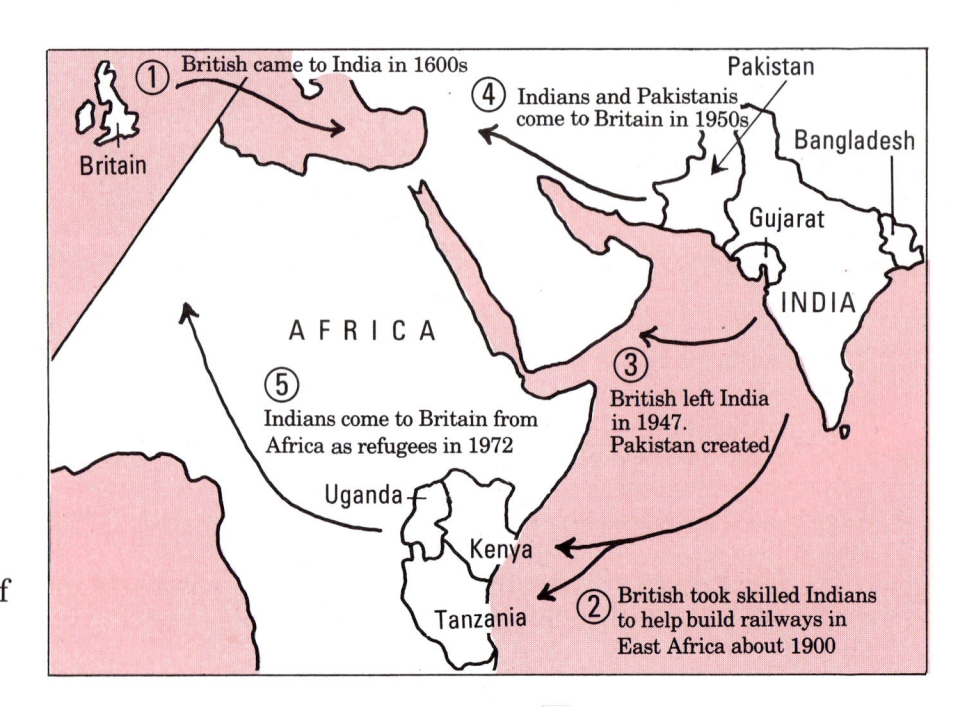

BEING A HINDU IN BRITAIN

Four of the pictures on these two pages were taken at a temple in Birmingham. There is no river or outdoor pool as there often is in India. The boys have taken off their shoes and wash their hands in the basin at the entrance to the temple.

The worshippers sit on the carpeted floor (p. 28). They sing and play music. There is a special puja today. The deity is carried shoulder-high round the temple. In India it would be a noisy crowded street procession involving all the neighbourhood. In the kitchen food is being prepared for several hundred people. Sharing a meal is important to Hindus.

One of the major differences between India and Britain is the weather! In India temple courtyards are open to the sky. Religious and social events like festivals, processions and weddings can happen out of doors. There is plenty of space.

At the Ganesh temple, on the right, in London, a man puts money in the box. Hindus give generously to the temple and to charity. This is part of dharma (their religious duty).

Many Hindu temples in Britain are church buildings or halls which have been bought and made into temples, like the ones shown here. They are more than a house for the gods and goddesses. They have become places where Hindus come to meet each other as well as to worship. People may travel long distances. Often (but not always) people who come from the same region in India, and therefore speak the same language, go to the same temple. Many temples have classes for adults and children to study the holy books and learn Indian music, languages and history.

Look at the picture on the right. A priest visits a home in Coventry to perform puja. In Britain, as in India, the home is still where many special events and acts of worship take place. Whenever there is a family event, relatives travel great distances to be together. Families help each other to pay for air tickets to and from India, Canada, America and other far-away places. Hindus visit India whenever they can afford to.

A sunny day in Battersea Park, London. And here IS a street festival which is organized every year by ISKON (International Society for Krishna Consciousness). This society started in 1979 with the teachings of a guru called Swami Prabhupada. It has many followers in Western countries. Its members worship the god Krishna. They wear orange or white robes and the men shave their heads. They often walk along Oxford Street (London) chanting 'Hare Krishna' and ringing bells. The other photograph shows the same festival being celebrated in Puri in India.

Here, in a Coventry temple, a family has arranged a special act of worship. The young woman is giving a drop of sacred Ganges water to each person. It is the anniversary of her grandmother's death and the family have opened a small copper jar which had water from the Ganges sealed in it. They brought it back from a pilgrimage in India. This is the moment they have chosen to share it with members of their temple.

1. Work with a partner. One of you is an elderly Hindu who came to Britain from Uganda. Your partner is a radio interviewer who wants to find out how and why you came to Britain. Using the map and information on p. 28, write down the script of the interview (or, if you can, tape record it).
2. Find photograph 2 on p. 3. Imagine you are a Hindu who has come from this village to live in London. Write down some of the differences and difficulties you may experience, especially in the way you practise your religion. (Think about the weather, space, expensive journeys, language, extra classes, being and looking 'different' in Britain.) The information and pictures on p. 29 will help you. Look also at pictures in chapters 1, 5, 6, 7, 9 and 11.
3. Hindus want to hold on to their links with India. Look at the photographs on this page. In what ways are links with India being kept alive in Britain? How will Hindu children who have always lived in Britain learn about how their religion is practised by their relatives in India? Discuss this quietly in groups of four.
4. On p. 31 are some sacred symbols and signs which Hindus may paint on their doorways or doorsteps. Copy and colour them.

NB If you are a Hindu reading this book, you will be able to help the others!

Tasks

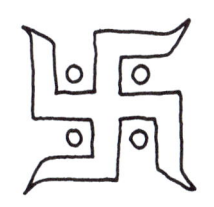

Note Try to work with a friend or a small group.

CHAPTER 1   Make a big wall map of India. Collect pictures (travel agents may help) and articles about India. Discuss them and stick them onto the map. Mark on it the places you read about in this book.

CHAPTER 2   Discuss beliefs about God and Hindu ideas about dharma, karma and samsara (rebirth). If possible ask a Hindu to come and join in. *Or* make a big collage of the sacred OM symbol, perhaps using coloured tissue-paper, wool, rice, shells or sequins.

CHAPTER 3   Make big copies of the drawings of the deities. Label their vehicles and the objects they hold. Make a wall frieze.

CHAPTER 4   Make masks and act out the story of Rama or Krishna. *Or* draw their stories cartoon style.

CHAPTER 5   Make figures of Hindus from pegs, wire, plasticine, clay or cardboard and scraps of material. Show their actions and gestures during worship (see also chapter 6 for ideas).
Listen to some Hindu religious music.

CHAPTER 6   Try to visit a Hindu temple. *Or* imagine you visited a temple yesterday with a Hindu friend. Write down what you did and saw and heard.

CHAPTER 7   Imagine you are one of the children in the havan picture. Write about all the excitement of that day. Describe what you saw and thought from when you woke up. How did you join in and help?

CHAPTER 8   Arrange a debate about the advantages and disadvantages of an 'extended' family. Tape record the debate.

CHAPTER 9   Prepare a questionnaire about religious rituals to mark times of birth, growing up, marriage and death. Try to fill in your questionnaire by speaking to people from more than one religion.

CHAPTER 10   Make a diary/sketch book. You live in Madras. You have just made a pilgrimage to Varanasi and Kedarnath. Write down how you travelled, what you did and what you saw. Draw pictures.

CHAPTER 11   Make a large copy on card of the calendar on p. 24 (not the writing in the middle). Draw a picture or symbol for each festival and fix a cardboard arrow in the middle with a paper fastener so that you can move it round.

CHAPTER 12   Find out and write about Mahatma Gandhi, one of India's most famous holy men.

CHAPTER 13   Imagine you are a Hindu who has recently come to live in Britain. Write a letter to your parents in India. Tell them about your local temple and how things are different here in Britain.

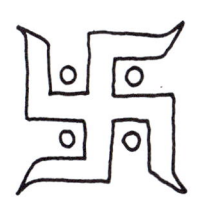

31

NOTES FOR TEACHERS

This book is intended for use with 9–14 year olds. No previous knowledge of Hinduism or of religious terminology is assumed. Hindu terms included in the Word List on p. 1 are printed in italics the first time they appear in the text. Aspects of history are included only in so far as they are needed to explain Hindu beliefs and practices today. The text is deliberately simple in vocabulary and presentation. Most of the questions at the end of each chapter can be answered with a single sentence but are designed to elicit fuller answers from the more able.

The chapters are self-contained and need not be used in numerical order. Pupils might work on different chapters on their own choosing. It is recommended, however, that before using this book a general introduction to Hinduism be given to the whole class. Ideally this should be done by using a video (such as *Hinduism through the Eyes of Hindu Children,* and, *Believe it or Not, Video I* available from RMEP) or filmstrip. Also of value would be a recording of Hindu religious music and singing and some Hindu artefacts such as carvings or pictures of gods and godesses, incense sticks, divas, bells, tabla and harmonium, a conch shell, mala (prayer-beads). Extra reference books about India and Hinduism from the library would be helpful and art and craft materials will be needed for the Tasks section. Some libraries and local R.E. resource centres are able to lend artefacts, and large calenders with dates of religious events and pictures of the deities are often available at temples and Indian shops. An increasing range of religious artefacts and posters may be purchased from Articles of Faith, Bury Business Centre, Kay Street, Bury BL9 6BU (tel. 061-705-1878). There is an excellent bookshop which also sells tapes of devotional music at the Institute of Indian Art and Culture at The Bhavan Centre, 4a Castletown Road, West Kensington, London W14 9HQ (tel. 071-381-3086).

It would be of great value, while this book is being studied, to arrange a visit to a temple and to encourage pupils to talk with Hindus about their religion, or to invite Hindus in to talk to the pupils. The optional Tasks list includes ideas for collaborative work and for research outside the classroom. The possibilities are obviously dependent to some extent on the location of the school and the facilities available.

ACKNOWLEDGEMENTS

The author wishes to thank Mr Ganesh Lal, Sri Mathoor Krishnamurti, Dr Helen Kanitkar and Eleanor Nesbitt for their help and critical advice. Thanks also to her son Tom and to her editor Mary Mears. And especial thanks go to Hansa Soni and her (extended) family for all that the author learned from them and for their hospitality in both Britain and India.

Thanks are also due to the following for the use of their photographs:

Barnaby's Picture Library: Cover picture (A. K. Chatterjee), pp. 3 (picture 2 – E. N. Issott), 4 (bottom – Ron Barlin), 12 (top – R. Dalmaine), 21 (ghat – H. Kanus), 30 (festival at Puri – Marie Mattson); Camera Press (London): pp. 5 (T. S. Nagarajan), 12 (bottom – Neha), 14 (top – Harry Miller), 16 (doorway – T. S. Nagarajan), 19 (top – T. S. Nagarajan), 20 (top – Stefan Richter, bottom – Jitendra Araya), 21 (horoscope – Stefan Richter, mundan ceremony – Jitendra Arya, sacred-thread ceremony – R. J. Chinwalla), 22 (Neha), 23 (mule trek – R. B. Bedi, pilgrims under tree – T. S. Nagarajan), 25 (blessing account books – R. J. Chinwalla, elephant – Harry Miller, Holi – Spaak), 26 (sanyasi – Harry Miller, procession – T. S. Nagarajan), 27 (astrologer – B. Bhansali); Delhi Press Information Bureau: pp. 3 (picture 1), 9 (crowns), 10 (masked dancers), 11 (Birla Temple), 19 (bottom), 25 (Durga statue); Sally and Richard Greenhill: pp. 8, 16 (kitchen shrine), 24; Ranchor Prime: p. 23 (Vrindavan); Westhill College, Birmingham: p. 23 (Varanasi).

The remaining photographs are by the author.

RELIGIOUS AND MORAL EDUCATION PRESS

An imprint of Chansitor Publications Ltd a wholly owned subsidiary of Hymns Ancient & Modern Ltd St Mary's Works, St Mary's Plain Norwich, Norfolk NR3 3BH
Copyright © 1993 Sarah Thorley
Corrected and reprinted 1993
Reprinted 1995
All Rights Reserved
ISBN 0 900274-55-7
Printed in Great Britain by
BPC Wheatons Ltd, Exeter for
Chansitor Publications Ltd, Norwich